The Developing **Artist**

HANON-FABER

The New Virtuoso Pianist

SELECTIONS FROM PARTS 1 AND 2

RANDALL FABER

T0057127

WITH TRANSFORMATIVE
WARM-UPS
TO DEVELOP
GESTURE AND VIRTUOSITY

Online Support
Scan the QR codes throughout the book
or visit **pianoadventures.com/qr/FF3035**

Production Coordinator: Jon Ophoff
Editor: Isabel Otero Bowen
Engraving: Dovetree Productions, Inc.

ISBN 978-1-61677-202-4

FABER
PIANO ADVENTURES®
3042 Creek Drive
Ann Arbor, Michigan 48108

Why This Edition

The exercises of Charles-Louis Hanon have been part of nearly every pianist's training for well over a century. However, since Hanon's publication in 1873, the piano has changed significantly. Longer strings, larger hammers, and heavier actions impose technical demands on today's pianist that were unanticipated at the time of Hanon. The finger technique prescribed by Hanon may have been adequate for the early keyboards of his time—the organ, harpsichord, fortepiano, and early pianoforte; but the modern grand requires an updated approach to piano technique. Hanon intended his 60 exercises of The Virtuoso Pianist to develop "agility, independence, strength, and perfect evenness in the fingers." Too often though, these exercises produce tension instead of dexterity. This edition provides vital preparatory exercises and practice routines that consistently develop the fine-motor skills for virtuosity at the modern piano.

A Chopin-era Broadwood, 50-65 grams of key weight

"Finger-building" exercises from the 19th century need to be retooled for the modern keyboard. Concert artists recognize that finger strength is subordinate to the coordinated use of fingers, wrist, and arm, which together harness efficiencies of gravity and gesture. Emphasis on alignment and gesture develops reliable control and a colorful palette of expression.

Developing pianists who rely only on finger technique typically reach an impediment in their technical progress. Failing to achieve fluency, they drive harder, practice longer, and over-exert the finger muscles while acquiring debilitating tensions. Practicing for finger strength is not only inefficient, it is likely to damage technique over the long term.

A modern grand, up to 110 grams of key weight

This edition revisits the Hanon exercises and presents them in a system that develops coordination, not tension. The revised sequence of exercises and the carefully conceived warm-ups for each help ensure appropriate relaxation and correct gesture. Not all of the original Hanon exercises have proven value. These and any potentially harmful exercises have been omitted. The Hanon-Faber edition provides a much needed practice routine that newly develops The Virtuoso Pianist.

FF30

TABLE OF CONTENTS

How to Practice

Begin with a week of practice on the Essential Motions, Gestures 1-3.

- Play by memory for attention to the *over* or *under* directions of the wrist half circle.

- Repeat with attention to the feel of each gesture, particularly the "walk out" and the "walk in."

- With repetitions over time you will automatize each gesture, so the movements flow from your fingers without concentration.

The Preparatory exercises (a-d) are more important and more effective than the Hands-Together exercises. Take your time with each "Prep" to master the feel of the fingertip as it contributes to and is supported by the gesture.

Observe these DOs (+) and DON'Ts (–).

- – Avoid the temptation of speed. The objective is to develop coordination.

- + Slow tempo with sensitivity to each finger is the prescription for progress.

- – Avoid pressure on the keybed after a key is played.

- + Play each finger with immediate relaxation after the impulse, yet without losing the hand structure. Imagine consecutive ripples or strong puffs of air.

If your hand or arm fatigues, revisit the gesture slowly. If you feel pain, you are either practicing too fast or playing incorrectly. Adjust to find the gesture that eliminates the pain, then take a break.

Expect and enjoy steady progress over time!

Gesture 1
Fingers 1-5 "Swoop"

This gesture traces the lower swoop of a wrist circle.*
It is effective for ascending passages in the right hand and descending passages in the left hand.

Gracefully drop into finger 1 and follow-through to finger 5.
Fingers 4 and 5 should actively "walk in" toward the fallboard, for a tall 5th finger knuckle.

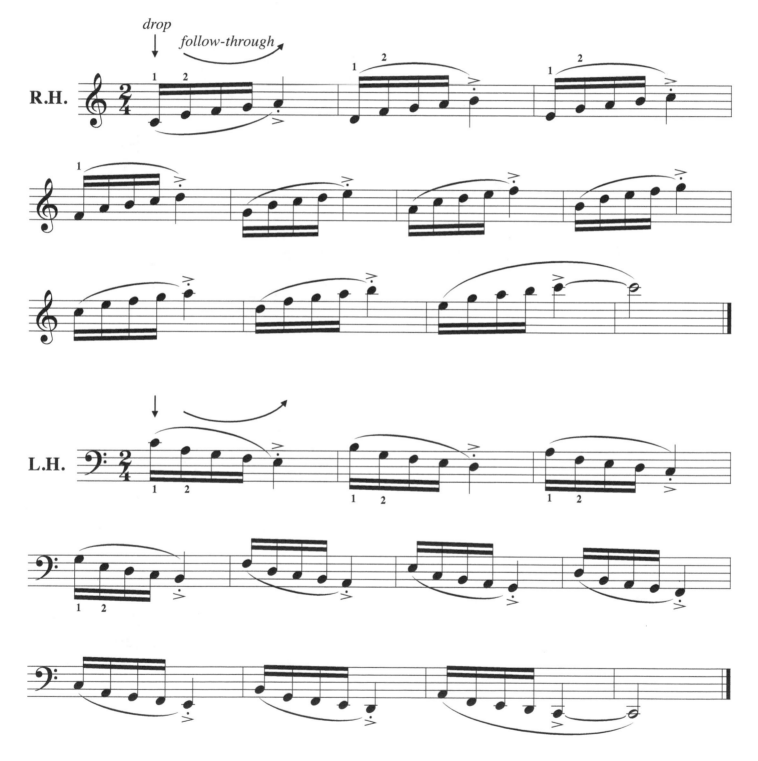

*See **Wrist Circle** and **Half Circle** in the Technique Glossary (page 64).
See also Piano Adventures® Technique & Artistry Book, Levels 3A and 4.

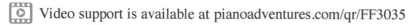 Video support is available at pianoadventures.com/qr/FF3035

Gesture 2
Fingers 5-1 "Arc"

This gesture traces the upper arc (over the top) of a wrist circle.*
It is effective for descending passages in the right hand and ascending passages in the left hand.

Use active fingers supported by a single impulse of the forearm.** Drive "over top" to a tall thumb.

*See Piano Adventures® Technique & Artistry Book, Levels 3A and 4.

**Use a forearm impulse that "walks in" toward the fallboard throughout the entire phrase.
  See Glossary (page 64).

FF30

Gesture 3
"Around the Corner"

This gesture facilitates a change of direction, a "turning the corner." At slow and moderate tempi, this implies coming around the outside and over top the circle. At fast tempi, it is a single, efficient impulse.

Drop* into finger 3, then make a "wrist circle" to complete the gesture. Phrase-off with a light thumb.

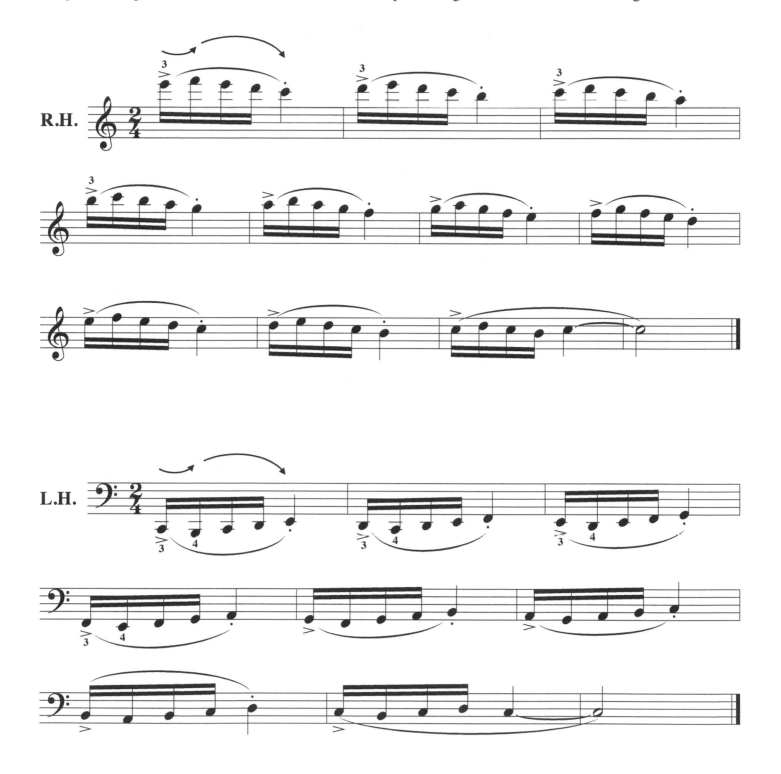

*Initiate with a drop of arm weight and release with a wrist float-off.

See Piano Adventures® Technique & Artistry Book, Levels 1 and 3A.

L.H. Prep 1

Use Wrist Circles: Swing *under*, then *over* with active fingers* 5 and 4.

*See Technique Glossary (page 64).

FF3C

R.H. Prep 1

Use Wrist Circles: Swing *under*, then *over* with active fingers 5 and 4.

1
Three Dimensions, No Tensions

Hanon, original form
The Virtuoso Pianist Part 1, No. 1

Feel a three-dimensional aspect of playing by using wrist circles as per the Prep exercises.

*Prepare the finger 5-4 skip by raising fingers 4-3-2 (L.H. for the first page and R.H. for the second page).

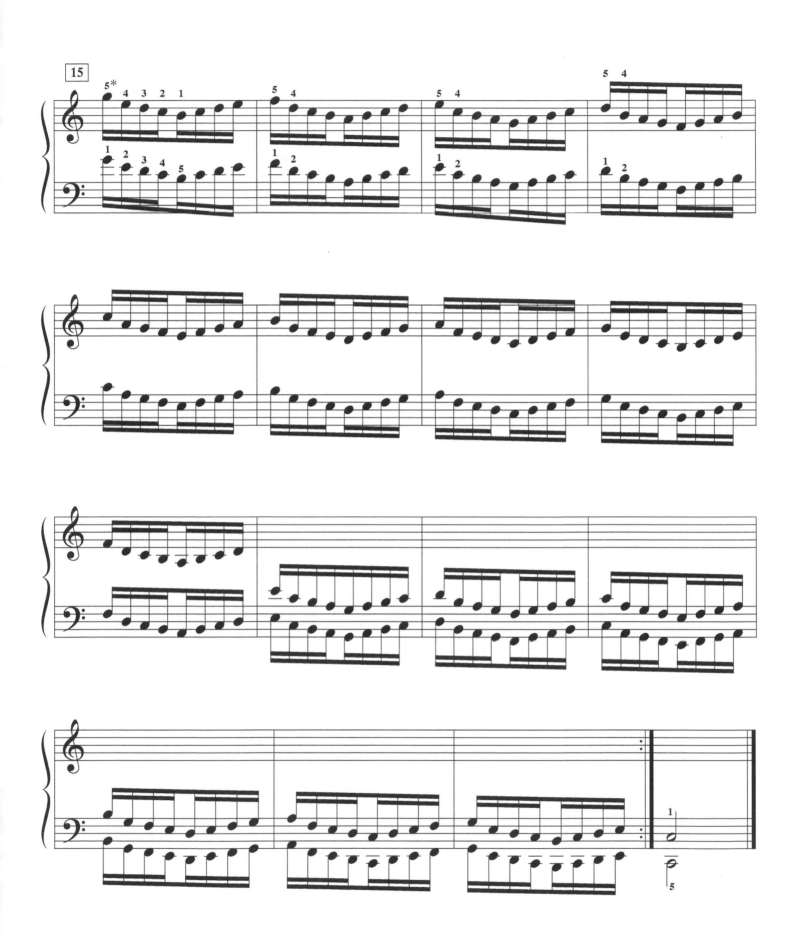

Set 1: Circles   11

L.H. Prep 2

Use a single wrist circle per measure to shape the phrase through the light staccatos.

FF3C

R.H. Prep 2

Use a single wrist circle per measure to shape the phrase through the light staccatos.

Set 1: Circles

2
Outside-Inside

Hanon, original form
The Virtuoso Pianist Part 1, No. 2

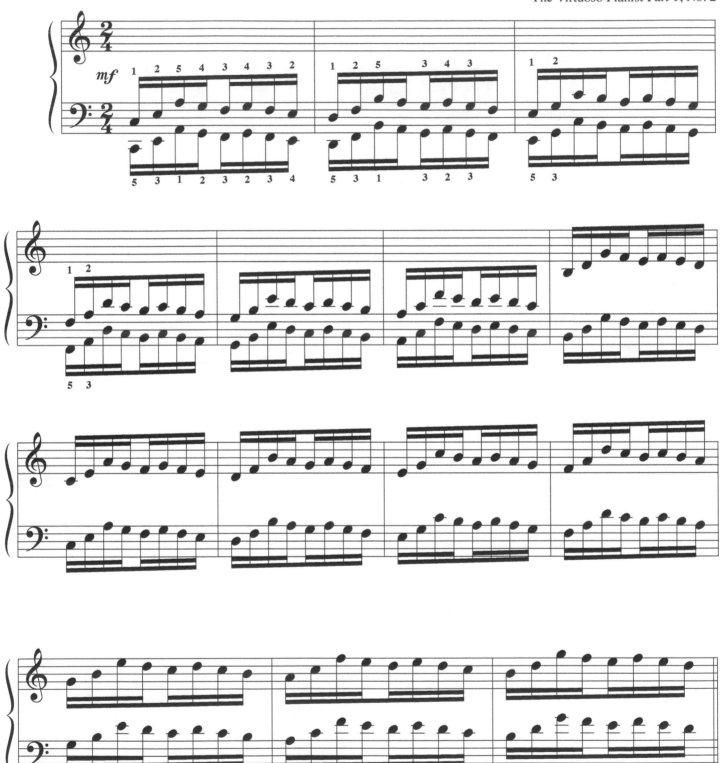

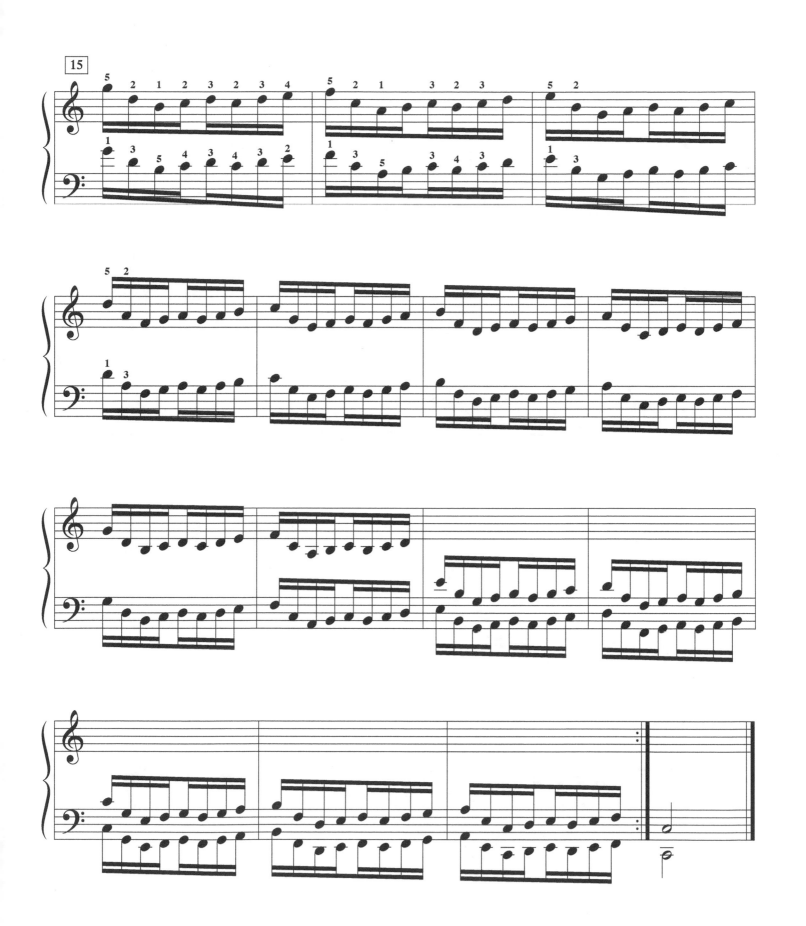

Set 1: Circles

L.H. Prep 3

Use a Light Thumb, followed by a half wrist circle going *over*.

R.H. Prep 3

Use a Light Thumb, followed by a half wrist circle going *over*.

3*
Over the Top

Hanon, original form
The Virtuoso Pianist Part 1, No. 4

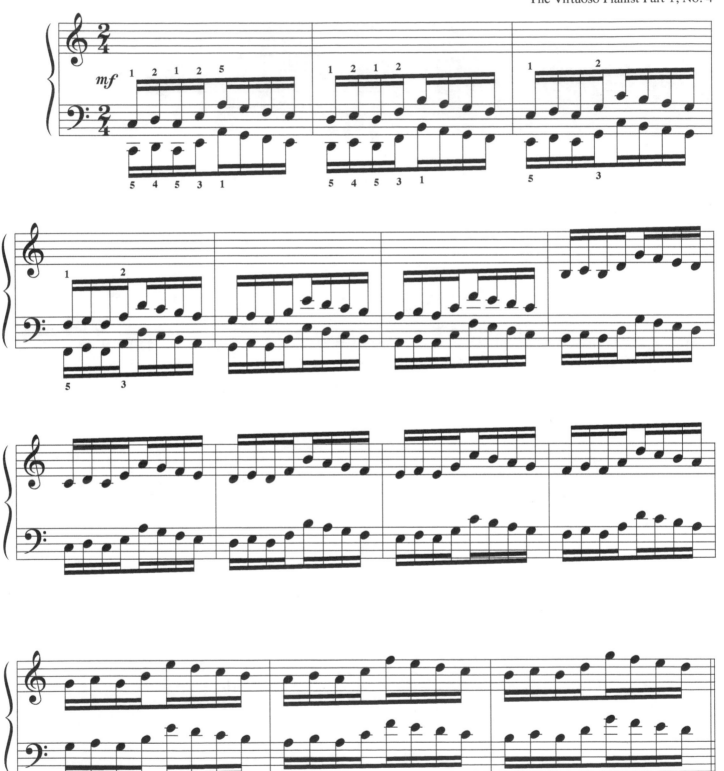

*The numbering reflects the optimized sequencing of this edition. Inefficient and potentially problematic exercises have been omitted.

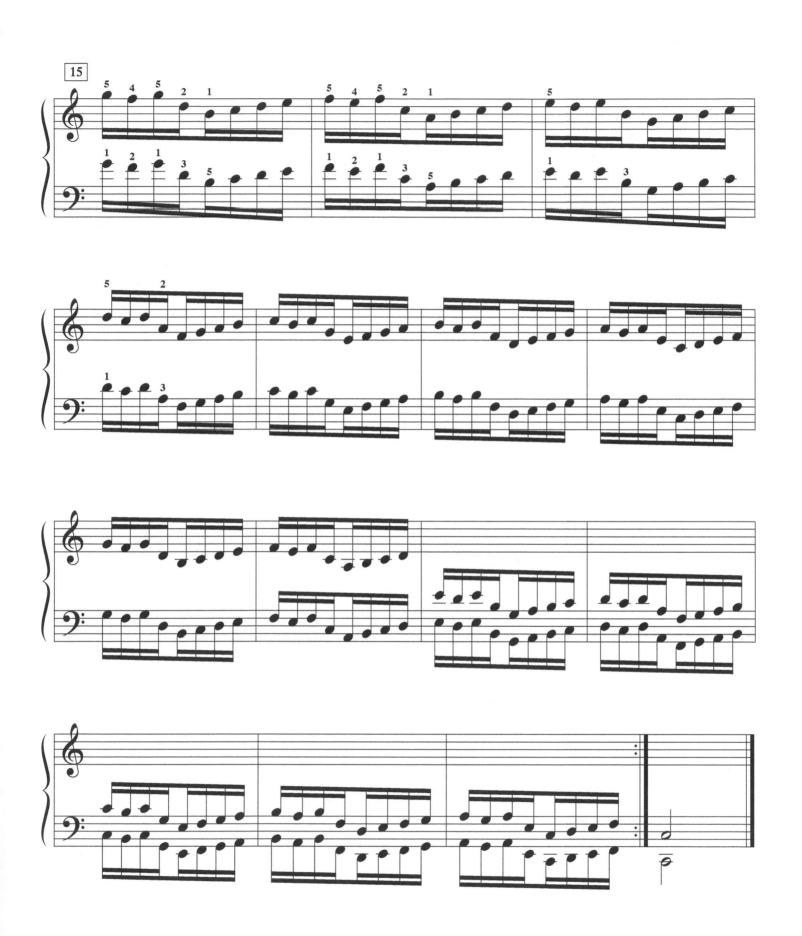

L.H. Prep 4

Use Rotation:* Toss to accented fingers 3 - 2 - 1.
Keep finger 5 close to the key; Swing back with 3 and 2 for the "toss."

*See Technique Glossary (page 64).

R.H. Prep 4

Use Rotation: Toss to accented fingers 3 - 2 - 1.
Keep finger 5 close to the key; Swing back with 3 and 2 for the "toss."

4
Wide Rotations

Hanon, original form
The Virtuoso Pianist Part 1, No. 6

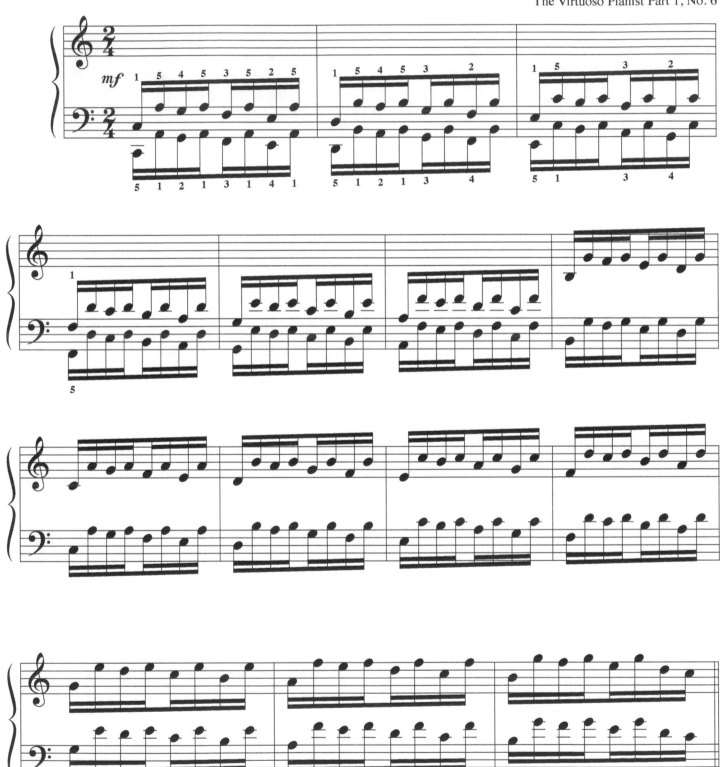

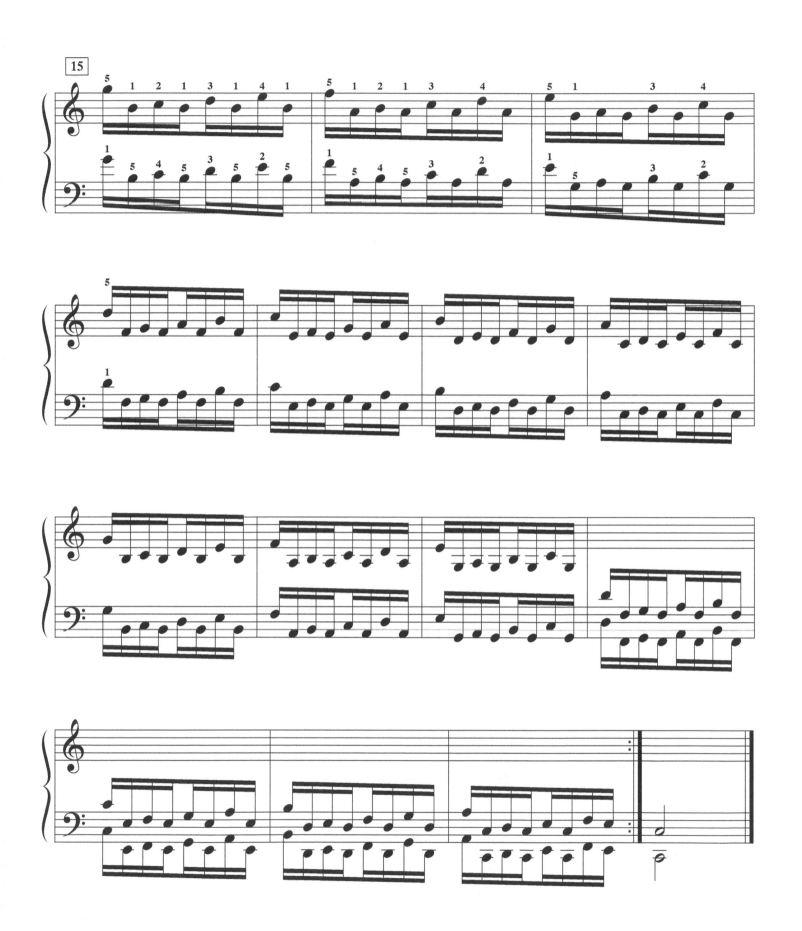

Set 2: Rotation

L.H. Prep 5

Use Rotation: Toss to accented finger 3.
Just preceding finger 3, pivot on the thumb to bring finger 3 high.

R.H. Prep 5

Use Rotation: Toss to accented finger 3.
Just preceding finger 3, pivot on finger 5 to bring finger 3 high.

5
Rotating 2nds

Hanon, original form
The Virtuoso Pianist Part 1, No. 5

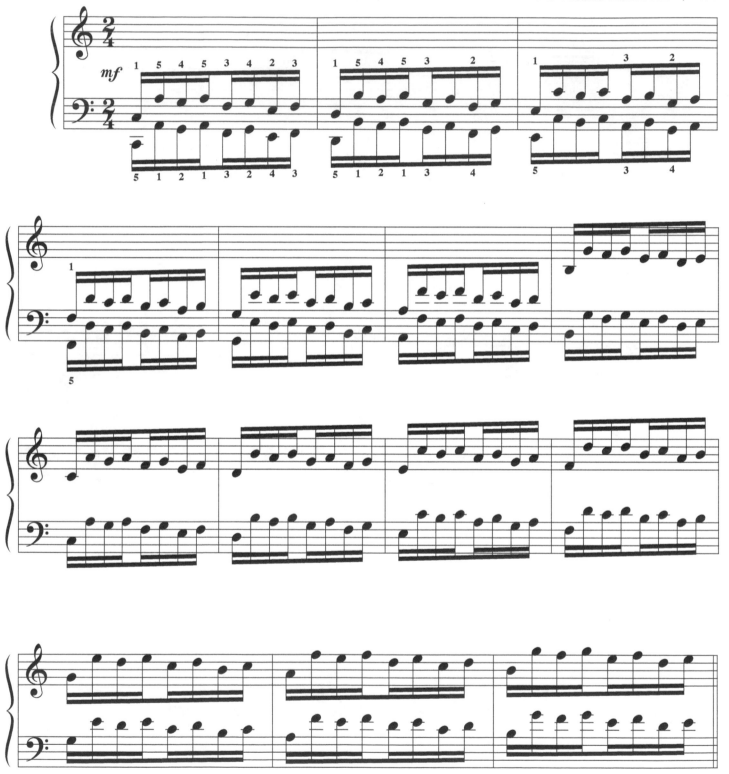

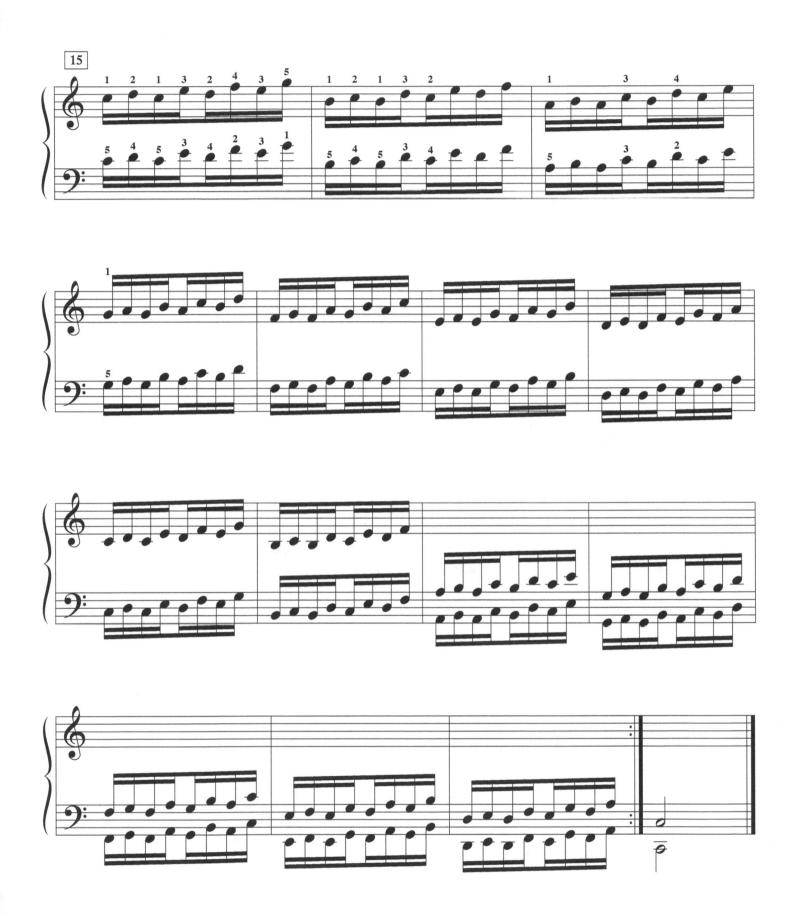

L.H. Prep 6

Use Wrist Circles: Swing briefly *under*, then continue *over* to the end of the measure. (Stay fluent through the repeated finger 2.)

R.H. Prep 6

Use Wrist Circles: Swing briefly *under*, then continue *over* to the
end of the measure. (Stay fluent through the repeated finger 2.)

6
Swirl to a Trill

Hanon, original form
The Virtuoso Pianist Part 1, No. 10

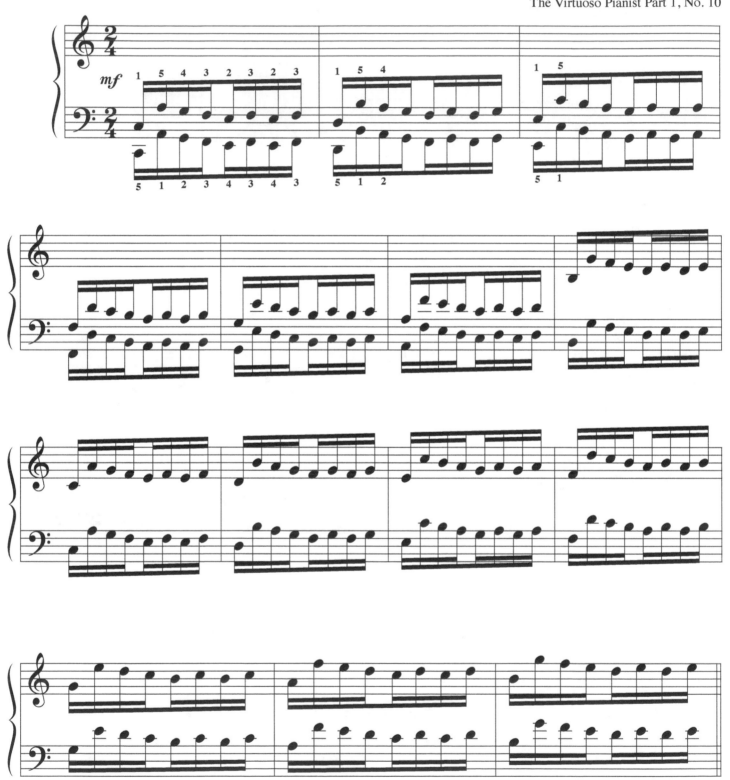

FF303

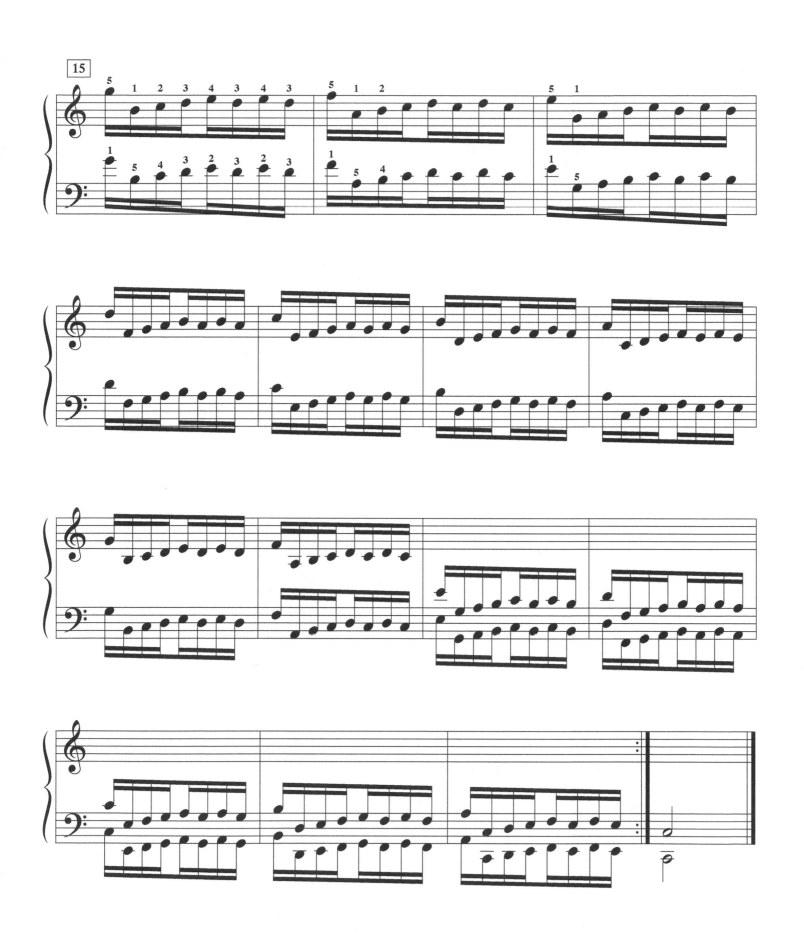

Set 3: Circles & Rotation

L.H. Prep 7

Use Wrist Circles: Swing *under*, then *over* with active finger 3 (and 2).

R.H. Prep 7

Use Wrist Circles: Swing *under*, then *over* with active finger 3 (and 2).

7
Accent Pairs

Hanon, original form
The Virtuoso Pianist Part 1, No. 8

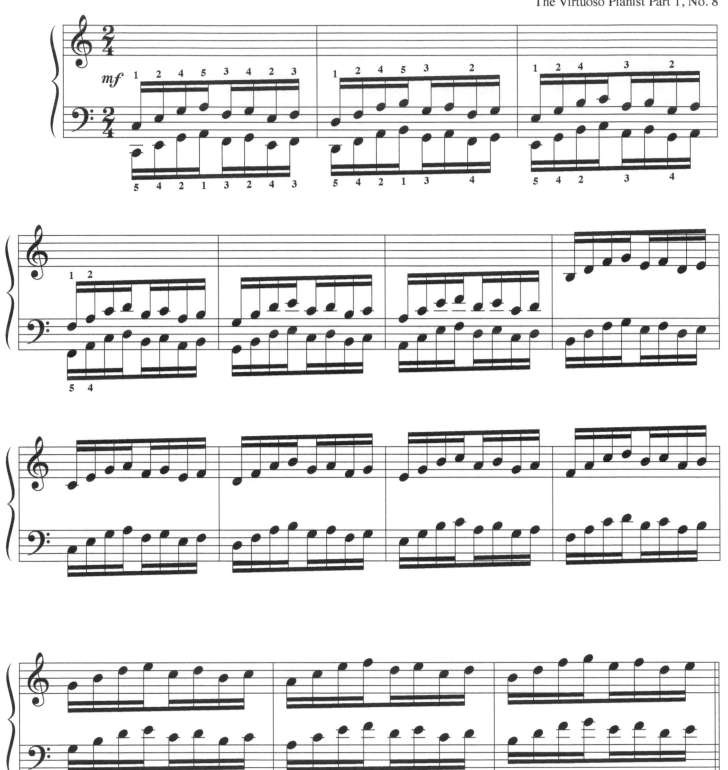

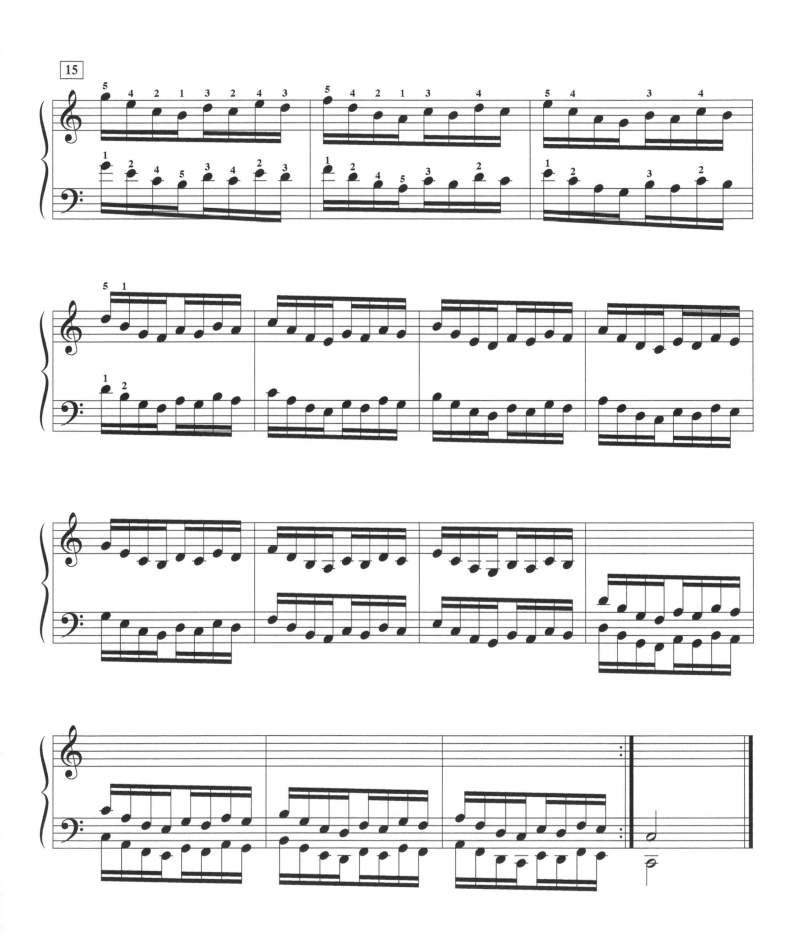

Set 3: Circles & Rotation

L.H. Prep 8

Use a Light Thumb. Flow over the bar line with soft, rapid fingerwork.

R.H. Prep 8

Use a Light Thumb. Flow over the bar line with soft, rapid fingerwork.

8
Rotating 3rds

Hanon, original form
The Virtuoso Pianist Part 1, No. 13

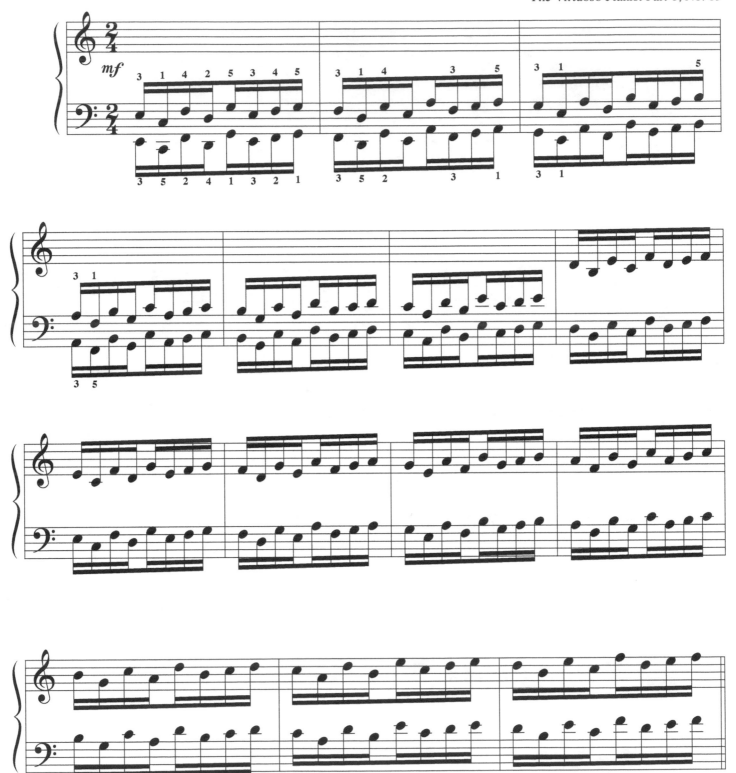

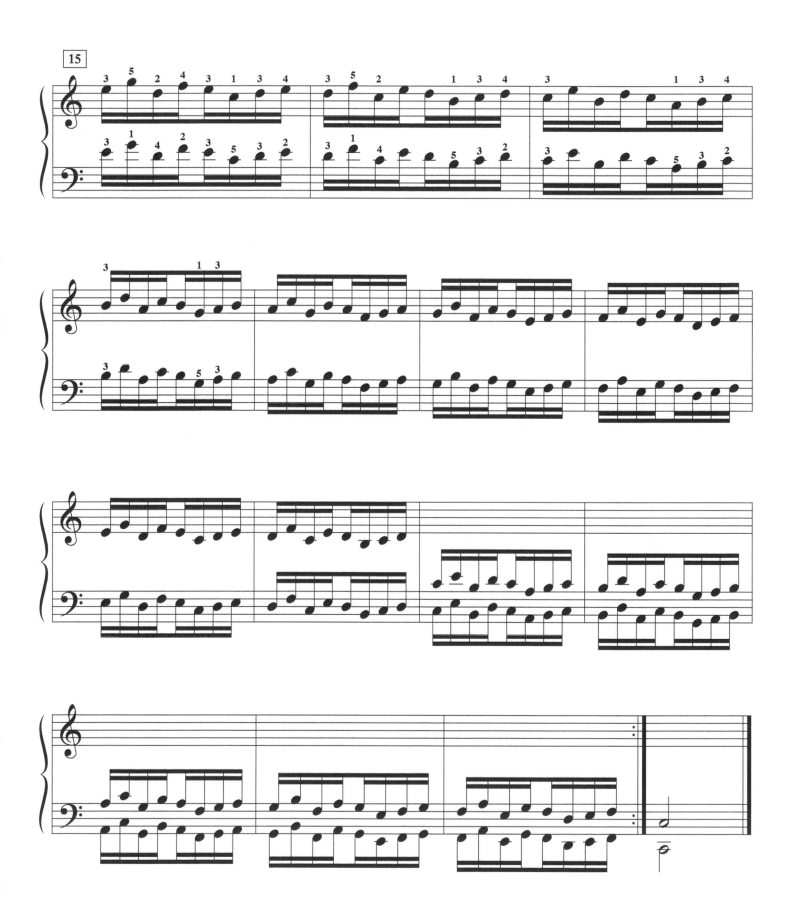

L.H. Prep 9

Use small wrist circles, keeping the hand closed.

FF303

R.H. Prep 9

Use small wrist circles, keeping the hand closed.

Set 4: Closing the Hand

9
Triple Skips

Hanon, original form
The Virtuoso Pianist Part 1, No. 7

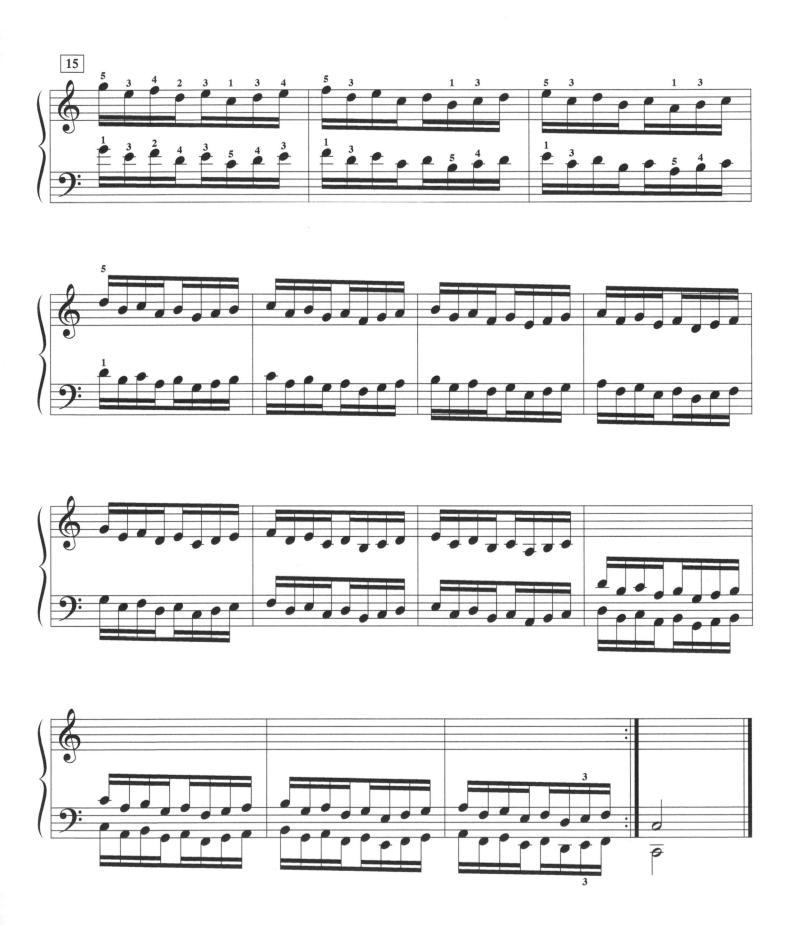

Set 4: Closing the Hand   43

L.H. Prep 10

Use a Wrist Circle: Drop into the downbeat with a half circle, rising to the end of the measure.

R.H. Prep 10

Use a Wrist Circle: Drop into the downbeat with a half circle, rising to the end of the measure.

Set 4: Closing the Hand

10
Turnaround

Hanon, original form
The Virtuoso Pianist Part 1, No. 14

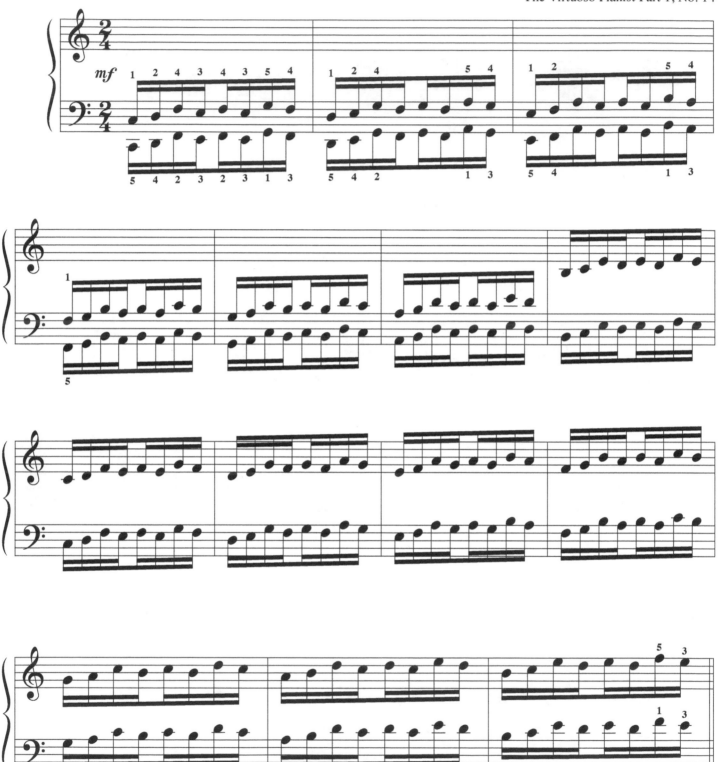

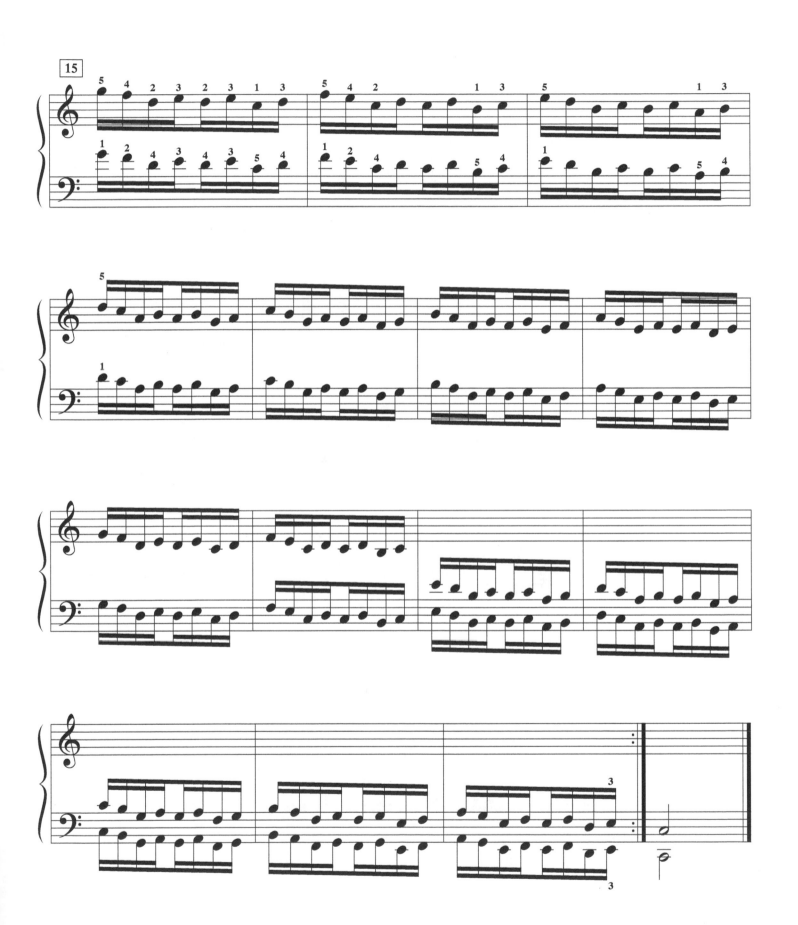

L.H. Prep 11

Use a Light Thumb and Wrist Circle:
Drop into the downbeat and rise to the end of the measure.

FF303

R.H. Prep 11

Use a Light Thumb and Wrist Circle:
Drop into the downbeat and rise to the end of the measure.

11
Walking 3rds

Hanon, original form
The Virtuoso Pianist Part 1, No. 15

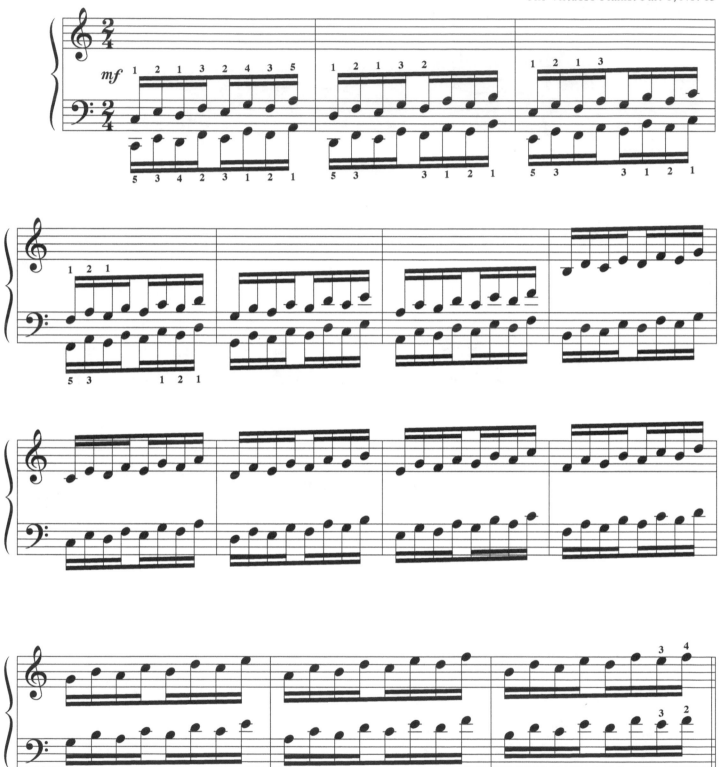

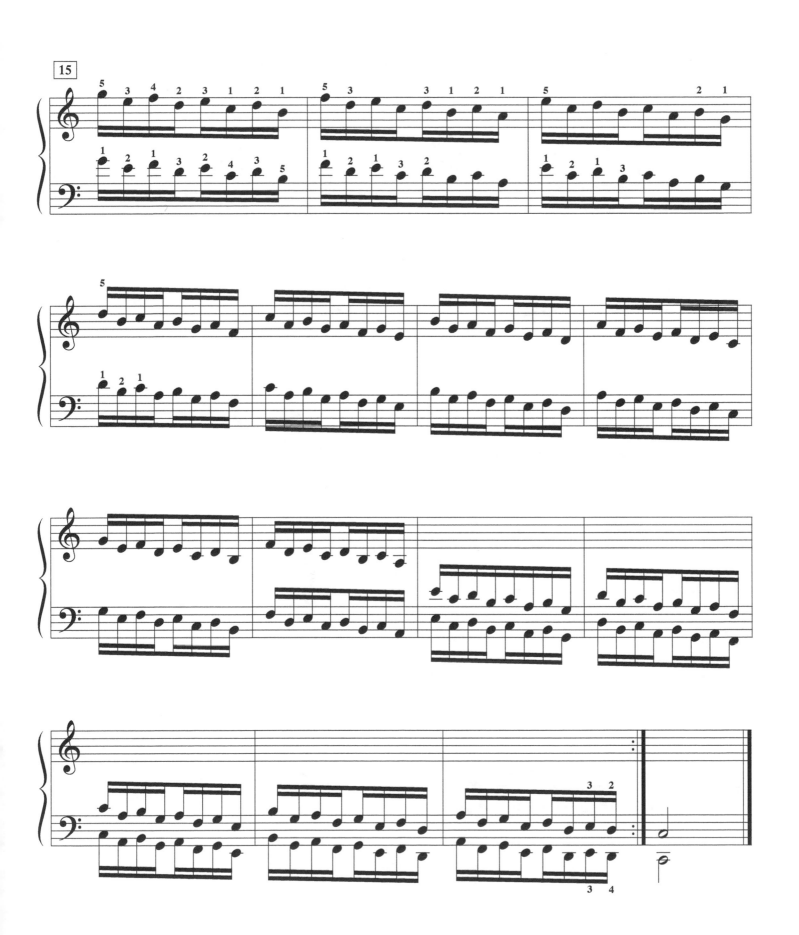

Set 5: Opening the Hand

L.H. Prep 12

Use a Wrist Circle to close the hand* for alignment on fingers 4 and 2.

*As you move through wide extensions, it is important to close the hand for relaxation.

R.H. Prep 12

Use a Wrist Circle to close the hand for alignment on fingers 4 and 2.

12
Open and Closed

Hanon, original form
The Virtuoso Pianist Part 1, No. 20

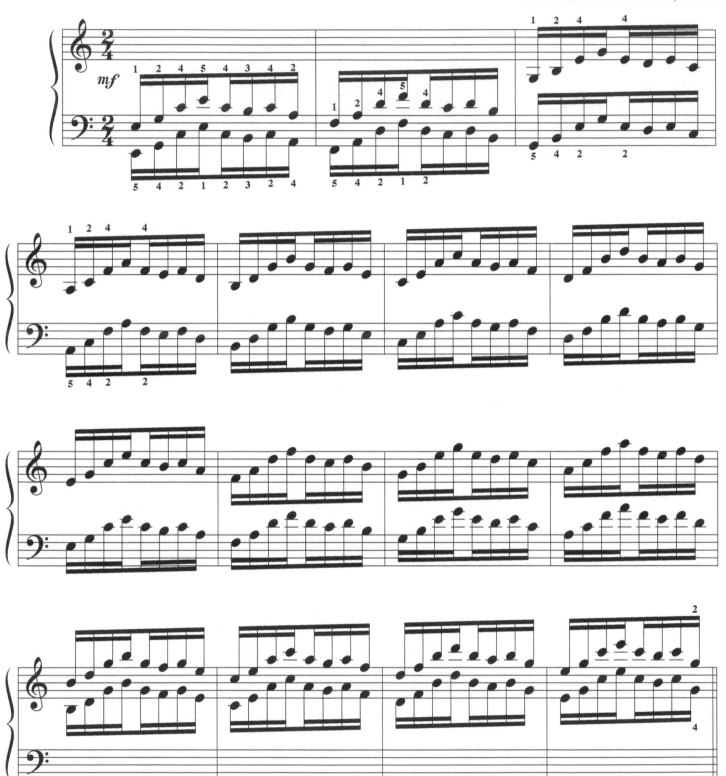

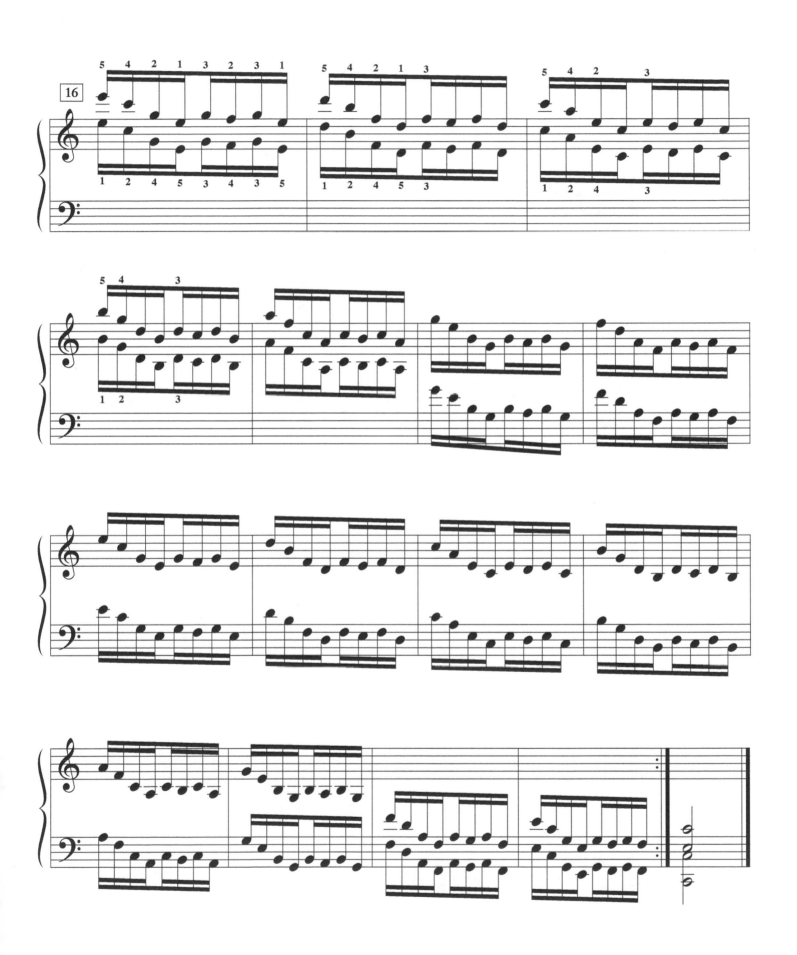

Set 5: Opening the Hand

L.H. Prep 13

Small wrist circles around fingers 1 and 5 are connected by a larger half circle,
as in Gestures 1 and 2 (pages 5-6).

R.H. Prep 13

Small wrist circles around fingers 1 and 5 are connected by a larger half circle,
as in Gestures 1 and 2 (pages 5-6).

13
Connecting Circles

Hanon, original form
The Virtuoso Pianist Part 2, No. 21

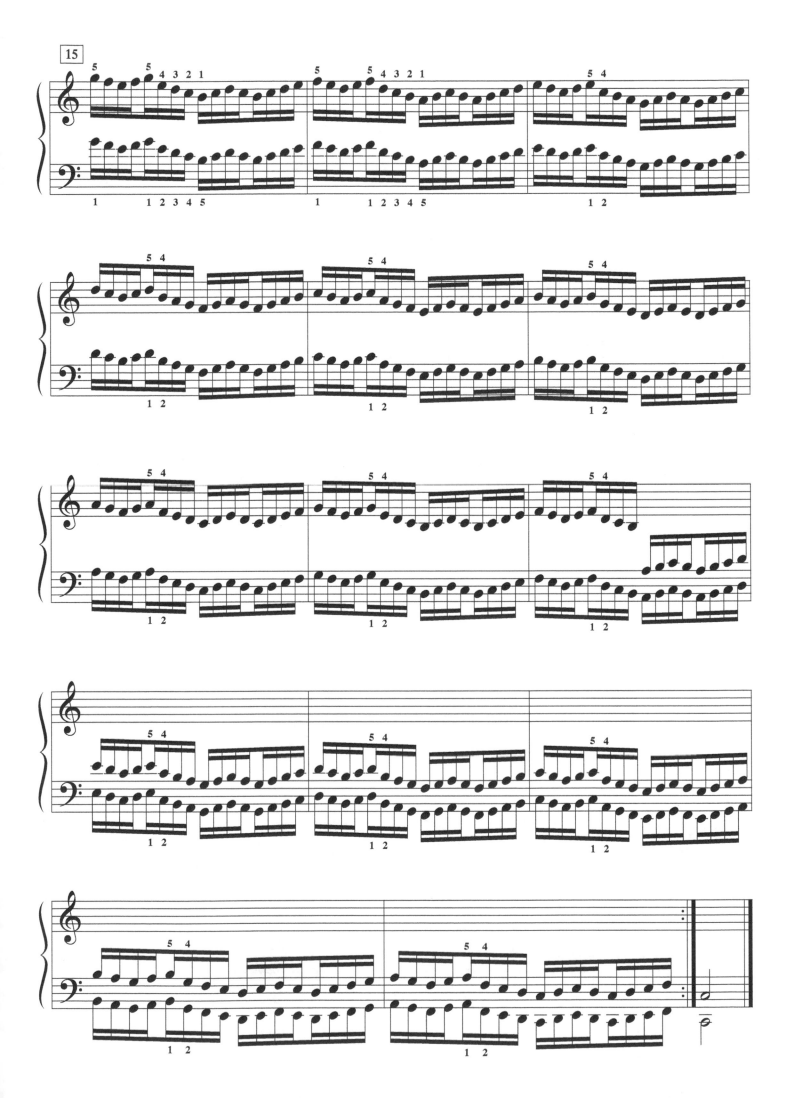

L.H. Prep 14

After rotation at the opening, use a slightly rising wrist with "walk-in" to relax the trill passage.*

*See Technique Glossary (page 64).

R.H. Prep 14

After rotation at the opening, use a slightly rising wrist with "walk-in" to relax the trill passage.

14
Finger Finale

Hanon, original form
The Virtuoso Pianist Part 2, No. 27

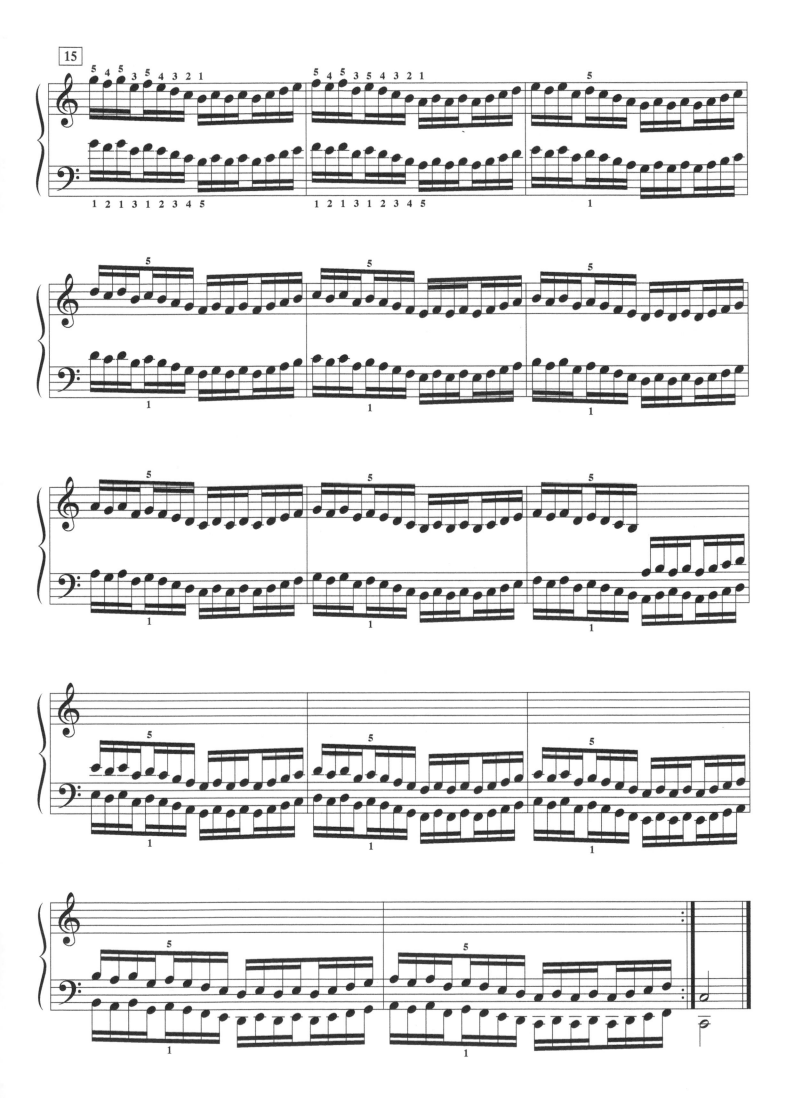

TECHNIQUE GLOSSARY

Active finger — Feel a spark at the fingertip, but hinge primarily at the large, base knuckle with wide motion of the finger.

Alignment — The arm, wrist, and large knuckle should be in a straight line to center arm weight into the fingertip.

Arm weight — Harness gravity by releasing the weight of both forearm and upper arm into the finger(s). This gives a rich tone with no fatigue.

Fallboard — The nameplate area at the back of the keys, which is usually also the hinged keyboard cover.

Forearm — The arm segment of elbow to wrist.

Half circle — Either the "swoop under" or the "arc over" segment of the wrist circle. See Gestures 1 and 2 (pages 5-6).

Impulse — A spark of energy initiated at the fingertip, from just behind the elbow, and from muscles in the back that propels the forearm toward the fallboard.

Rotation — A pivot of the forearm as if turning a key. Also called "forearm rotation." Rotation is either toward the outside of the hand, as if pivoting on the thumb with tall, falling fingers (pronated hand); or, rotation in the direction of the thumb, as if pivoting on finger 5 with a high thumb (supinated hand). Note that many fingers are raised together along with the hand. This provides a stored energy which not only releases to play the next key, but also rebounds to play another key on the return. Two or more notes are played with minimal expenditure of energy and without tension.

Walk in — Motion toward the fallboard, whereby each fingertip becomes more curved, as in playing fingers 3-4-5, or the "over arc" of Gesture 2, playing fingers 5-1.

Walk out — A brief pull toward the body, away from the fallboard; usually from thumb through finger 2 as in the "under swoop" of the wrist circle. See Gesture 1.

Wrist circle — A circular tracing of the wrist that aligns the forearm and large knuckle over the finger as it plays. (The elbow traces a small concentric circle.) Hands-together circles will be in mirror image, typically swooping under for fingers 1 to 5 and over for fingers 5 to 1. (L.H. in clockwise motion; R.H. counter clockwise.)

L.H.   **R.H.**

FF303